You're Tall in the Morning But Shorter at Night

AND OTHER AMAZING FACTS ABOUT THE HUMAN BODY

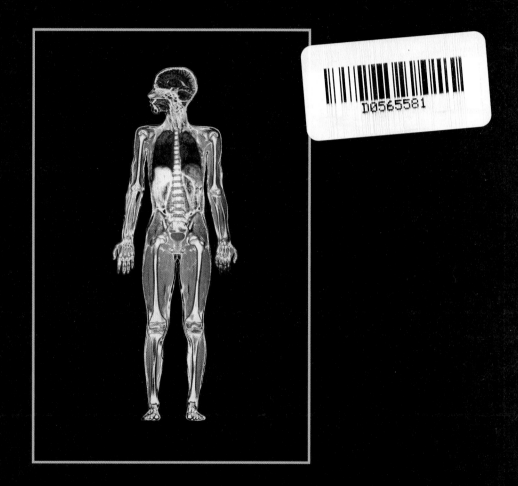

by Melvin and Gilda Berger

SCHOLASTIC INC.

New York   Toronto   London   Auckland   Sydney
Mexico City   New Delhi   Hong Kong   Buenos Aires

ISBN 0-439-62536-X

12 11 10 9 8 7 6 5 4 3 2 1   4 5 6 7 8 9/0

Printed in the U.S.A.
First trade printing, August 2004
Interior art by Rémy Simard
Design by Janet Kusmierski
Photo research by Sarah Longacre

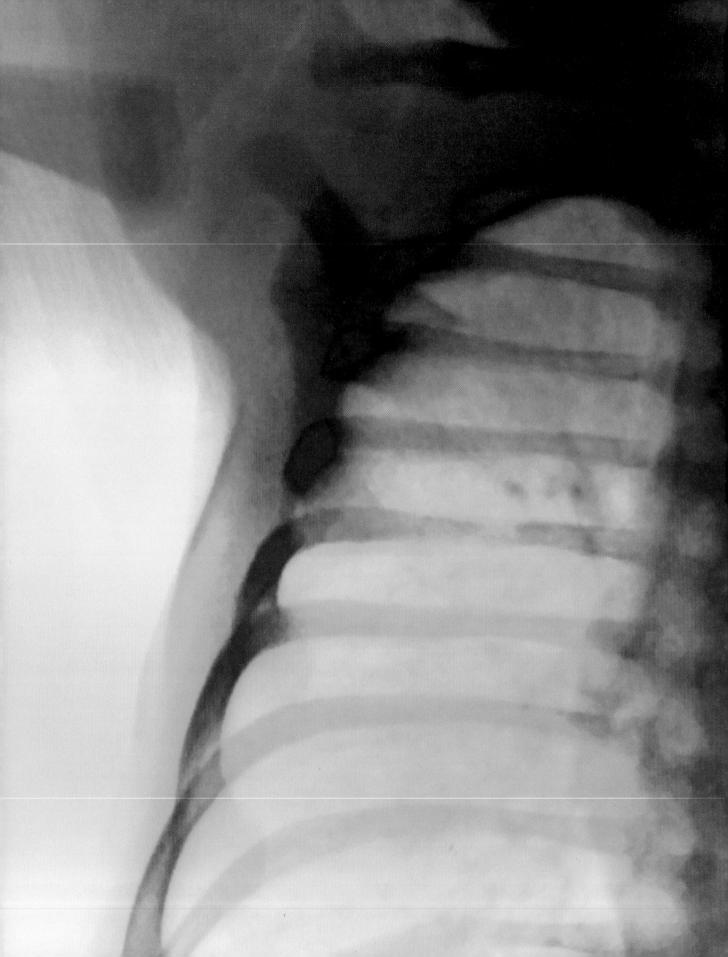

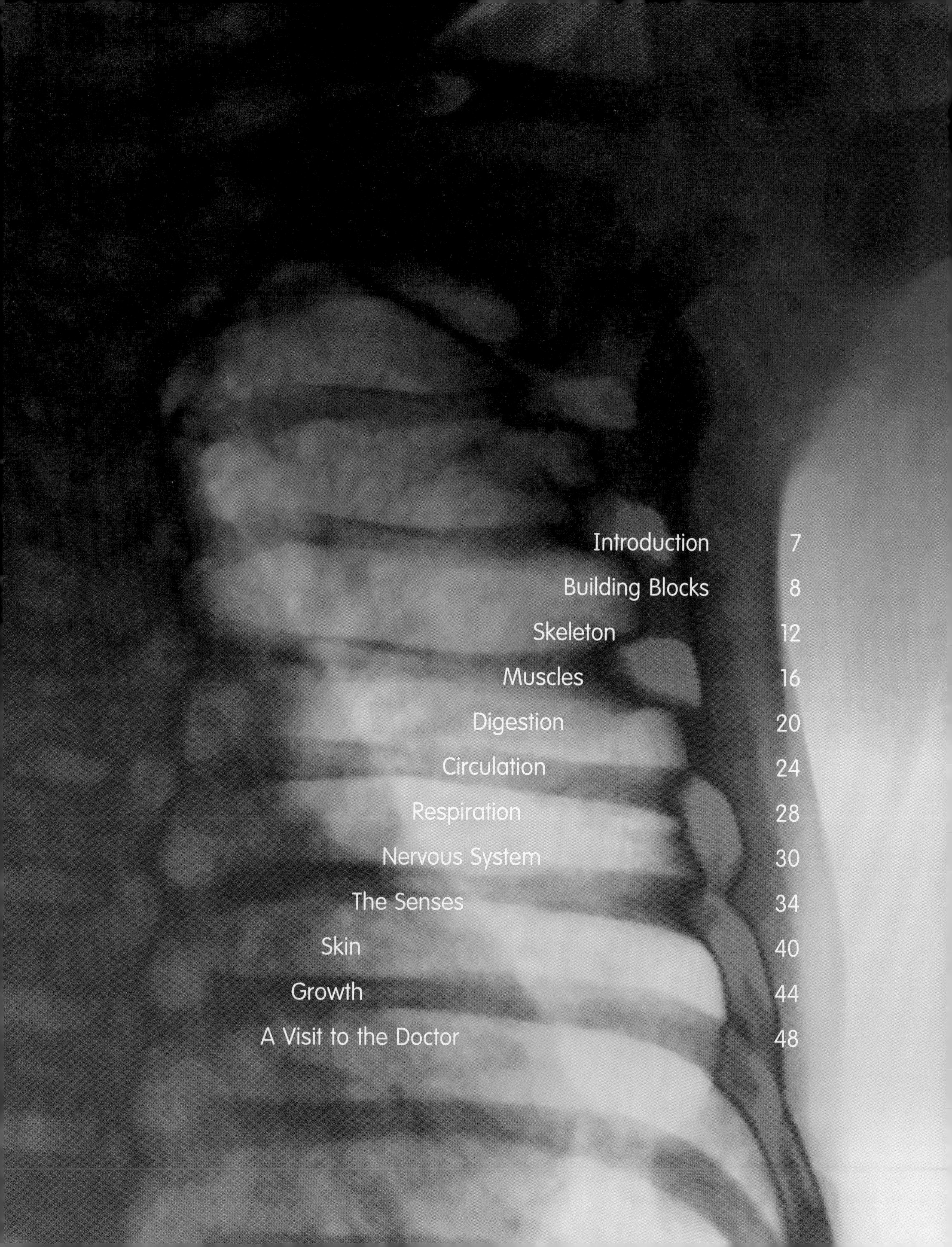

KEY TO ABBREVIATIONS

cm = centimeter

cm^2 = square centimeter

g = gram

kg = kilogram

km = kilometer

kph = kilometers per hour

l = liter

m = meter

mph = miles per hour

t = metric ton

INTRODUCTION

This book is about the main parts of your body. It tells you how they work and the important jobs they do.

The hard parts inside your body are bones. They make up your skeleton and protect your insides.

Muscles are joined to bones. They let you move about.

Your stomach and intestines help to break down the food you eat.

Inside the chest are your heart and lungs. The heart pumps blood all around the body. The lungs fill up with air when you breathe in and empty when you breathe out.

Your brain controls all your thoughts and feelings. It receives messages from your eyes, ears, and other senses. It also sends messages to your muscles.

How well do you know your body? Did you know that

- you use 200 muscles each time you take a step,

- your heart is the size of your fist,

- feelings come from your brain, not your heart,

- most of your ear is inside your head, and

- your digestive system is about 33 feet (10 m) long?

Read on, and be amazed by more Speedy Facts about the human body!

BUILDING BLOCKS
Cells

Your body is made up of about 100 trillion tiny bits of living material called cells. Each cell is a building block of the body. Many millions of cells make up each body part.

But not all cells are alike. Cells have many different shapes because they have many different jobs to do. Bone cells support your body. Nerve cells send messages to, from, and inside your brain. Muscle cells tighten and relax so you can move.

Most cells are too small to see without a microscope. Yet each cell is alive—taking in food and getting rid of wastes.

BONE CELL

Speedy Fact 1

Your body contains about 200 different kinds of cells.

Speedy Fact 2

Most cells are tiny. About 40,000 red blood cells can fit inside this letter *O*.

Speedy Fact 3

The longest cells in the body are the nerve cells. They can be 40 inches (100 cm) long.

Speedy Fact 4

Every minute, about 3 billion cells die and are replaced in your body.

8

Tissues

Since cells are so tiny, huge numbers of similar cells join together to do one kind of job. Such groupings of cells are called tissues.

You have four main kinds of tissues in your body. Muscle tissues tighten and relax to move different body parts. Nerve tissues carry signals from one part of your body to another. Epithelial (ehp-uh-THEE-lee-uhl) tissues form your skin and the linings of your mouth, lungs, stomach, and other body parts. Connective tissues join together and support various parts of your body.

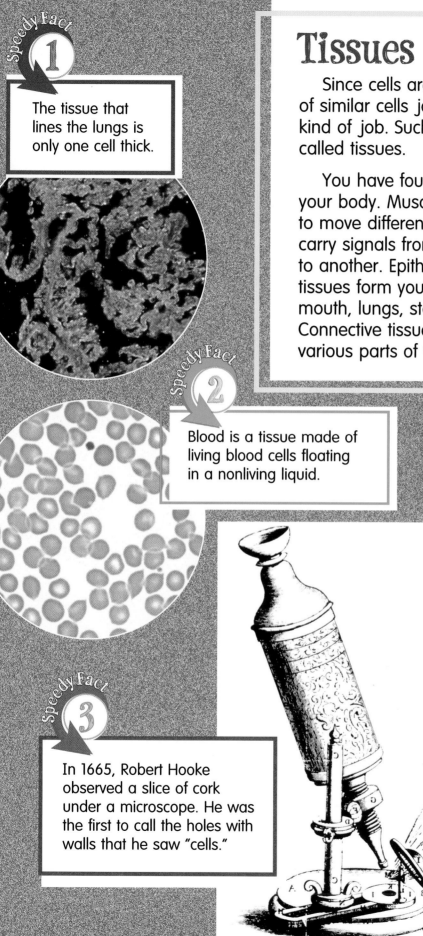

Speedy Fact 1

The tissue that lines the lungs is only one cell thick.

Speedy Fact 2

Blood is a tissue made of living blood cells floating in a nonliving liquid.

Speedy Fact 3

In 1665, Robert Hooke observed a slice of cork under a microscope. He was the first to call the holes with walls that he saw "cells."

Organs

Two or more kinds of tissues that work together to do a certain job form an organ. Your heart, for example, is an organ made up of muscle tissue, nerve tissue, and connective tissue. Its job is to pump blood throughout the body.

The human body has about 50 organs, including the eyes and the skin. Organs inside your body include the heart, brain, stomach, and intestines.

Speedy Fact 1
The largest organ is the skin.

Speedy Fact 2
In 2000, the most common transplanted organ in the U.S. was the kidney.

Speedy Fact 3
Many organs, such as the eyes and ears, are on the left and right sides of the body and are almost exactly alike.

Speedy Fact 4
Organ transplants are becoming more common.

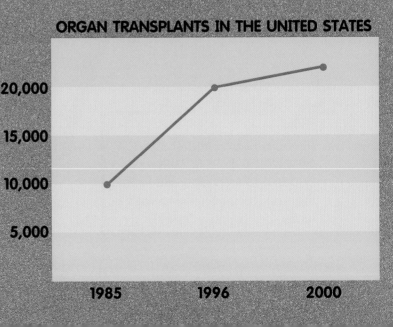

ORGAN TRANSPLANTS IN THE UNITED STATES

20,000	
15,000	
10,000	
5,000	

1985   1996   2000

Speedy Fact 1

Hunger pains are what you feel when your stomach is empty and the stomach muscles are churning.

Speedy Fact 2

Signals can speed through the nervous system as fast as 200 miles per hour (321.8 kph).

Speedy Fact 3

The warmth you feel after exercise comes from the slow burning of food in the cells of your muscular system.

Organ Systems

Groups of organs work together to form organ systems. There are 12 organ systems in the human body. They include the skeletal, muscular, digestive, circulatory, respiratory, and nervous systems.

Each system carries out a major function. The organs of the digestive system, for example, digest the food you eat. Among its organs are the stomach, small intestine, and large intestine. These organs change food into a form that the cells can use for growth, repair, and energy.

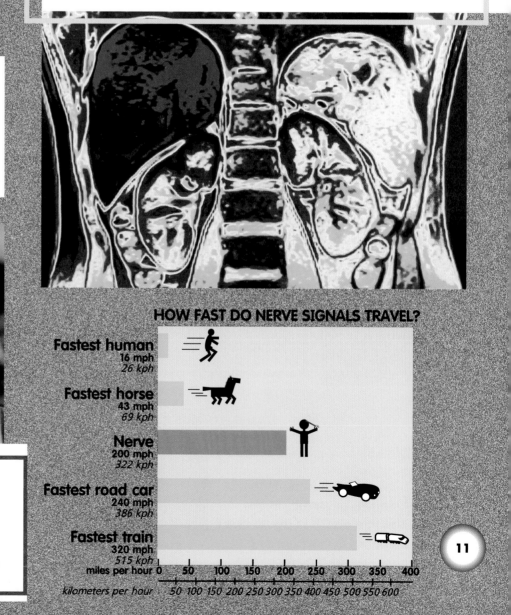

HOW FAST DO NERVE SIGNALS TRAVEL?

	miles per hour	kilometers per hour
Fastest human	16 mph	26 kph
Fastest horse	43 mph	69 kph
Nerve	200 mph	322 kph
Fastest road car	240 mph	386 kph
Fastest train	320 mph	515 kph

miles per hour 0 50 100 150 200 250 300 350 400

kilometers per hour 50 100 150 200 250 300 350 400 450 500 550 600

SKELETON
Bones

Your bones are part of your skeleton. One of their most important jobs is to hold you up, or support you. Without bones, you could not stand or sit upright. You wouldn't be able to walk, run, skate, or swim, either.

Your bones also protect the important organs of your body. Your skull bone is like a hard hat that protects your brain. Your 12 pairs of ribs are like a strong cage for your heart and lungs.

Speedy Fact 1

You were born with 300 bones. By the time you graduate from high school, some bones will have joined together and you'll have only 206 bones.

Speedy Fact 2

The thighbone, or femur, is the biggest bone in the body. An adult femur is about 20 inches (51 cm) long—half the length of a baseball bat—and up to 2 inches (5 cm) thick.

Speedy Fact 3

More than half the bones in your body are in your hands and feet.

Speedy Fact 4

The shortest bone is the stapes, or stirrup, in the middle ear. It is about one tenth of an inch (0.25 cm)— the size of a grain of rice.

Speedy Fact 5

Humans have the same number of neck bones as giraffes and mice. Luckily, our neck bones are smaller than those of giraffes and bigger than those of mice.

A Closer Look at Bones

The solid outside part of bone is very hard. It is made of living bone cells packed tightly together into rings. The inside of most bones is a hollow canal. In some bones, nerves and blood vessels run through this center.

Other bones are filled with a yellow or red jellylike substance called marrow. Yellow marrow is mostly fat and is found in the long bones of the arms and legs. Red marrow is found in the ribs, shoulder blades, pelvis, and breastbone. Marrow produces blood cells for the body.

Speedy Fact 1

The hard outside of your bones is a little less hard than the enamel on your teeth.

Speedy Fact 2

Bones can stand a pressure of 24,000 pounds (10,886 kg) per square inch (6.5 cm^2). That's about four times stronger than steel.

Speedy Fact 3

The red bone marrow in your body makes about 2 million new red blood cells every second of the day.

Speedy Fact 4

Dogs chew on animal bones to get the yellow marrow.

Joints

Bones are stiff and don't bend. But most bones are connected to each other by movable joints.

You can swing your leg back and forth because of the hinge joint in your knee. You can turn your head from side to side because of the pivot joint at the top of your backbone. And you can twist and turn your body because of the ball-and-socket joints in your hips.

Speedy Fact 1

You have more than 200 joints in your body. There are about 40 joints in your hand alone.

Speedy Fact 2

You are tallest in the morning because the joints in your backbone pull slightly apart when you are lying in bed. During the day, gravity squeezes the bones together and you can lose as much as 1 inch (2.5 cm) of height.

Speedy Fact 3

The joints in your shoulder and elbow let you move your arms more freely than you can move your legs.

Speedy Fact 4

Your skull is made of eight separate bones. They are joined together by fixed joints that are locked in place.

Ligaments and Cartilage

Your bones are held together at the joints by straplike fibers called ligaments. When you bend a joint, the ligaments stretch. When you straighten the joint, the ligaments spring back like rubber bands.

Bones often rub against each other in the joints. A smooth, bluish-white pad over the bone ends, called cartilage, keeps the joints slippery and able to move easily. Cartilage also cushions bones against shock.

Speedy Fact 1

When ligaments tear, twist, or stretch, you get a sprain.

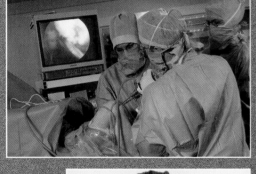

Speedy Fact 2

Before birth, your skeleton is all cartilage. As you grow, the cartilage changes into bone.

Speedy Fact 3

Your bones grow by adding thin layers of cartilage at the ends, which slowly change into bone.

Speedy Fact 5

Instead of bones, sharks have cartilage inside their bodies. The cartilage bends and lets the sharks twist and turn in the water.

Speedy Fact 4

You can feel cartilage in your ears and in the tip of your nose.

MUSCLES
Movers and Shakers

Your muscles move the bones of your body. The 600-plus muscles in your body are like ropes that pull on the bones so that you can move.

You control most of your muscles. These muscles are called the skeletal, or voluntary, muscles. Every time you pick up a pen or scratch your nose, skeletal muscles do the job. You also have smooth, or involuntary, muscles. These muscles work by themselves and take care of breathing, digestion, and so on.

Speedy Fact 1

The tongue is your most movable muscle.

Speedy Fact 2

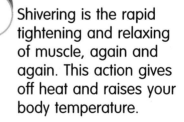

Your strongest muscles, for their size, are the muscles on the sides of your mouth. They let you bite with a force of 150 pounds (68 kg).

Speedy Fact 3

Shivering is the rapid tightening and relaxing of muscle, again and again. This action gives off heat and raises your body temperature.

Speedy Fact 4

The busiest muscles are around your eyes. They tighten and loosen about 100,000 times a day.

Speedy Fact 5

Nearly half your body weight is muscle, including most of your arms, legs, chest, neck, and face.

Tendons

Tendons are bundles of white, tough, stringy fibers that attach muscles to bones. By pulling on the tendons, the muscles move the bones.

Tendons are either round or flat. They are like ligaments, except not as elastic. You can feel your Achilles' tendon, the strongest of all tendons, on the back of your ankle. It connects your calf muscles to your heel bone.

Speedy Fact 1

You have 20 tendons in each wrist.

Speedy Fact 2

Fingers have tendons but no muscles. The muscles that move fingers are in your hand and forearm.

Speedy Fact 3

Doctors can sew a cut tendon together. It takes about six weeks or more for the tendon to heal.

Speedy Fact 4

A tendon can withstand a pull of 57 tons (58 t) per square inch (6.5 cm²).

Muscles at Work

Most muscles work in pairs. If you lift your forearm slowly, the biceps muscle on top of your arm grows shorter and thicker. At the same time, the triceps muscle under your arm gets longer and thinner. When you lower your forearm, the biceps muscle becomes longer and the triceps muscle becomes shorter.

Muscles can pull but not push. That's why they most often work in pairs.

Speedy Fact 1

In 1985, Lamar Grant of the United States set a record by lifting weights totaling 660 pounds (300 kg). That was five times as much as he weighed!

Speedy Fact 2

Excercise doesn't give you more muscles. It just makes your muscles stronger.

Speedy Fact 3

It takes eight muscles to move your thumb—four in your arm and four in your hand.

Speedy Fact
1

When you're cold or scared, tiny smooth muscles in your skin form goose bumps that make your hairs stand up.

Muscles on Their Own

Smooth muscles work on their own, or automatically. You don't have to think about getting them to move. Smooth muscles in your blood vessels, for example, push blood through your body. Others help you swallow food or move your ribs in and out so you can breathe.

The muscles in your heart work like smooth muscles even though they look like skeletal muscles. Unlike skeletal muscles, healthy heart muscles never tire.

HOW MANY MUSCLES DOES IT TAKE?

To take a step
200 muscles

To talk
72 muscles

To frown
43 muscles

To smile
15 muscles

To pick up a pencil
12 muscles

0 20 40 60 80 100 120 140 160 180 200

Speedy Fact 2

Smooth muscles in the linings of the stomach and intestine move the food along in waves.

Speedy Fact 3

A person telling a lie has small, smooth-muscle reactions that can be picked up by a lie detector.

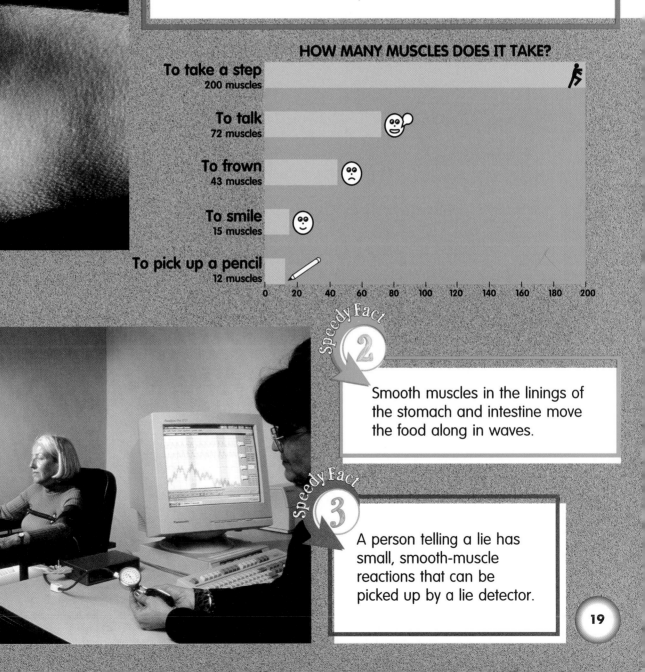

19

DIGESTION
Mouth

In order for cells to live and grow, they must have food. Digestion breaks down the food you eat into microscopic bits called molecules. The molecules are small enough to pass through the walls of the cells.

You start digestion by breaking off pieces of food with your front teeth. Your back teeth crush, grind, and mash the food into small bits. As you chew, saliva flows into your mouth, making the food soft and moist. Saliva also contains a chemical that starts to break apart the food.

Speedy Fact 1

Every day about a quart (0.9 l) of saliva flows into your mouth.

Speedy Fact 2

When saliva enters your mouth, it is free of germs. Once you start chewing, the saliva picks up millions of germs from inside your mouth.

Speedy Fact 3

Just the sight or smell of food can "make your mouth water," which means saliva is entering your mouth.

Esophagus and Stomach

When you swallow food, the pulpy mass enters a long tube called the esophagus (i-SOF-uh-guhss). Wavelike movements of the smooth muscles in the walls of the esophagus push the food into your stomach.

Juices from the lining of your stomach mix with the food. The juices soften the food. Chemicals in the juices break the food down into smaller and smaller bits. At the same time, muscles in the stomach wall churn and mix the food. Most food stays here between three and five hours.

Speedy Fact 1

Muscles move food through the esophagus—even if you're upside down. It takes about 10 seconds for food to get from your mouth to your stomach.

Speedy Fact 2

An empty stomach looks like the letter *J*. When filled with food, it becomes 20 times larger.

Speedy Fact 3

The digestive juices in the stomach are strong enough to dissolve metal.

Speedy Fact 4

A burp is a bubble of gas from your stomach. It can be air you swallowed, fizzy bubbles from soda, or gas that formed as you digested your food.

Small Intestine

Connected to the stomach is the small intestine. Here, more juices pour into the food. They change all the food that can be digested into molecules that are small enough to be used by your cells.

Lining the wall of the small intestine are millions of "mini-fingers" called villi. From the villi, the food molecules pass into tiny blood vessels, known as capillaries. The blood carries the molecules to cells all over the body.

Speedy Fact 1

The small intestine is about 22 feet (7 m) long and 1 inch (2.5 cm) wide.

Speedy Fact 2

It takes four to six hours for food to move through the small intestine.

Speedy Fact 3

Stomach rumbles come from your small intestine, not your stomach. Smooth muscles in the walls of the small intestine push, squeeze, churn, and knead the food—making quite a racket!

Speedy Fact

1

The large intestine is shorter and thicker than the small intestine.

Large Intestine

You cannot digest some of the food you eat. This undigested material moves to the wider part of your intestine known as the large intestine, or colon. The leftovers from digestion collect here. In time, you pass this solid waste out of your body.

Water and other liquids from the food go into the blood. The blood carries the fluid to the kidneys and bladder. When the bladder is full, you excrete the fluid waste as urine.

Speedy Fact

2

There are more germs in the large intestine than anywhere else in the body. The billions of germs form a thick layer on the wall of the large intestine.

Speedy Fact

3

Food takes up to two days to pass through your body.

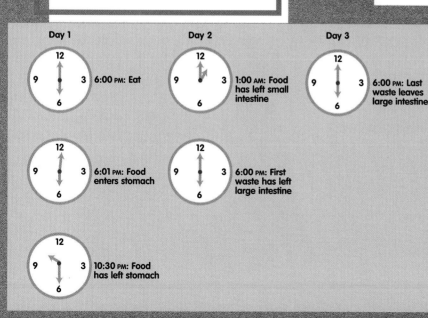

Day 1
12 9 3 6 — 6:00 PM: Eat
12 9 3 6 — 6:01 PM: Food enters stomach
12 9 3 6 — 10:30 PM: Food has left stomach

Day 2
12 9 3 6 — 1:00 AM: Food has left small intestine
12 9 3 6 — 6:00 PM: First waste has left large intestine

Day 3
12 9 3 6 — 6:00 PM: Last waste leaves large intestine

23

CIRCULATION
'Round and 'Round It Goes

Your heart and blood vessels make up the circulatory system. This system keeps blood flowing to all parts of your body.

The heart pumps the blood into tubes called arteries. The arteries connect with smaller arteries, and then to very thin tubes called capillaries. From the capillaries, the blood flows back to the heart through other tubes called veins.

Arteries take the blood away from the heart. Veins bring it back. 'Round and 'round the blood goes, never stopping, never leaving the blood vessels. English physician William Harvey discovered the circulatory system in 1628.

Speedy Fact 1

The human circulatory system is 62,500 miles (100,000 km) long. If stretched out, the blood vessels would stretch two times around the earth.

Speedy Fact 2

Your arm or leg "falls asleep" when you block its blood circulation by not moving it or by holding it in a cramped position.

Speedy Fact 3

Blood makes a round-trip in about one minute.

Heart

Your heart is a hollow, muscular organ about the size of your fist. It contains two separate pumps, side by side. Each pump has an upper part and a lower part. Your heart pumps between four and five thousand gallons (15,141 and 18,927 liters) of blood every day—enough to fill an oil truck.

The two upper parts receive blood flowing into the heart. The lower part on the right then sends blood to your lungs to pick up oxygen from the air in the lungs. The lower part on the left pumps the oxygen-rich blood out through an artery to the rest of your body.

Between the upper and lower parts are little flaps called valves. The valves make sure the blood flows in only one direction.

Speedy Fact

1

Doctors use a stethoscope to listen to the heart.

Speedy Fact

2

Your heart is in the center of your chest, but you feel your heartbeat on the left side. That's because the bottom of the heart leans to the left, where the stronger lower pumps are located.

Speedy Fact

3

The heart weighs slightly less than one pound (0.5 kg).

Speedy Fact

4

Your heart usually beats between 60 and 70 times a minute. It slows down when you rest and speeds up when you exercise.

Speedy Fact

5

By age 70, your heart will have beat at least 2 billion times.

Pulse and Blood Pressure

Most arteries and veins are deep inside your body. But in a few places, they are just beneath your skin. You can see some veins as thin blue lines under your skin. You can feel some arteries as the blood surges through them. Each beat of your heart causes a surge, or pulse, of blood.

The heart forces the blood to flow under great pressure through the blood vessels. Blood pressure is a measure of the force of the blood pushing against the walls of the blood vessels.

Speedy Fact 1
You can feel your pulse by holding a finger lightly on your wrist.

Speedy Fact 2
Capillaries are thinner than a hair on your head. Their walls are only one cell thick.

Speedy Fact 3
The main arteries are about as thick as your thumb. The largest is the aorta, which carries blood away from the heart.

Speedy Fact 4
Blood pressure in the aorta is so great that if it is cut, the blood will spurt out 6 feet (1.8 m) high.

Speedy Fact 5
A black eye occurs when a punch or other blow breaks the blood vessels around your eye and leaves blood trapped under the skin.

Blood

Blood flows through your body like a great river. It brings food molecules from your intestines to all of your cells. It carries oxygen from the lungs to the rest of your body. And it takes away all the waste products.

Your blood has four main parts: red blood cells, which take in oxygen from your lungs and bring it to other parts of your body; white blood cells, which mostly fight the germs that cause disease; plasma, the thick, sticky, liquid part of your blood that carries the red cells and the white cells; and platelets, tiny disks that help to stop bleeding from a cut.

Speedy Fact 1

A little more than half of the blood is plasma. Plasma is 90 percent water. The other 10 percent includes some 100 dissolved chemicals.

Speedy Fact 2

Every drop of blood contains red blood cells, white blood cells, and platelets.

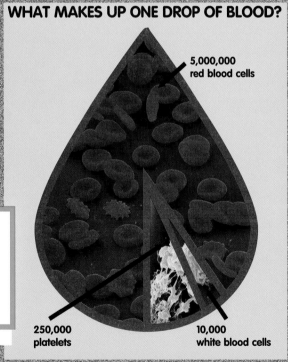

WHAT MAKES UP ONE DROP OF BLOOD?

5,000,000 red blood cells

250,000 platelets

10,000 white blood cells

Speedy Fact 3

The amount of blood in your body depends on your size.

Speedy Fact 4

After someone gives a pint (0.5 l) of blood for a transfusion, it takes the body about 10 days to rebuild its supply.

RESPIRATION
Breathing In

Every few seconds, day and night, asleep or awake, air flows in through your nose and down a long tube: the windpipe. At its lower end, the windpipe divides, sending the air into your two lungs.

The air contains oxygen, which the body cells need to burn the food you eat for energy. The oxygen seeps through the walls of the lungs and into the blood. As the blood flows throughout the body, the oxygen goes out of the blood and into the cells.

If your lungs and windpipe are in good health, the doctor hears a whistling, sighing sound. A bubbling sound may signal an infection.

Speedy Fact 1

The walls of the lungs are just one cell thick.

Speedy Fact 2

At rest, you breathe in every four seconds. After running a race, you breathe twice a second— about eight times as fast.

Speedy Fact 3

An adult's lungs can hold up to 5 quarts (4.7 l) of air.

1 gallon (3.8 l)   1 quart (0.9 l)

Speedy Fact 4

Asthma (AZ-muh) occurs when muscles in the lung narrow the airways, making breathing difficult. Special sprays help relax the muscles and open the airways.

Speedy Fact 5

Eating or drinking too much or too fast may make a muscle in your chest pull down with a jerk and force you to take a quick breath. HICCUP!

Breathing Out

The burning of the fuel in your cells creates a gas called carbon dioxide, which your body does not need. The gas moves out of the cells and into the blood. The blood then carries the carbon dioxide back to your lungs. Breathing out sends the waste carbon dioxide out of your lungs and into the air.

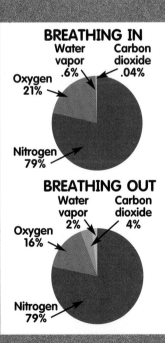

Speedy Fact 1

All air contains some carbon dioxide. But when you breathe out, your breath has ten times as much carbon dioxide as the air you breathe in.

Speedy Fact 2

Scrunched inside your chest, your lungs are no bigger than a supermarket bag. If you could spread them flat, however, they would cover half a tennis court.

BREATHING IN

Water vapor .6%
Carbon dioxide .04%
Oxygen 21%
Nitrogen 79%

BREATHING OUT

Water vapor 2%
Carbon dioxide 4%
Oxygen 16%
Nitrogen 79%

Speedy Fact 3

Sneezing sends breath out of your mouth at 100 miles per hour (161 kph).

Speedy Fact 4

By the time you are 70 years old, you will have breathed in and out more than 500 million times.

NERVOUS SYSTEM
Busy Network

Your nervous system is like a busy telephone network inside your body. Day and night, millions of messages flow in and out. At the center of the nervous system are your brain and spinal cord.

Some incoming messages carry information about what is happening in and around your body. Some outgoing messages carry orders telling your body what to do. Other outgoing messages automatically control the work of your heart, lungs, stomach, and other organs.

Speedy Fact 1

The skull is like a helmet that guards the brain against bumps and bruises. The bones of the spine protect the spinal cord.

Speedy Fact 2

The nervous system reaches almost everywhere in the body—even inside teeth and bones.

Speedy Fact 3

A hard blow on the head may make you "see stars." The flashes are due to disturbances in the normal work of the nervous system.

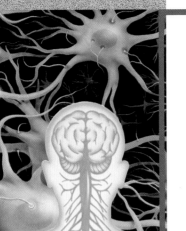

Nerves

All the messages to and from your brain and spinal cord travel through millions of nerves. The nerves branch out from the brain and spinal cord to every part of your body.

Nerves are long fibers built of nerve cells, or neurons. Each neuron is also very long. Its ends touch many other neurons. Where they touch, tiny electrical signals jump from neuron to neuron.

Speedy Fact 1

Your body has about 50 miles (80.5 km) of nerves.

Speedy Fact 2

Signals speed through neurons at about 350 feet (10,500 cm) a second. They carry as many as 2,500 messages in that time.

Speedy Fact 3

Twelve pairs of nerves travel from the brain to the head and neck. Thirty-one pairs run from the spinal cord to the rest of the body.

Speedy Fact 4

Unlike most other cells, neurons are not replaced if they are badly damaged.

Speedy Fact 5

A neuron may contact as many as 1,000 other neurons.

Brain

The brain is the master control center of the nervous system and of the whole body. It is the main receiver and sender of messages from the nerves. But it does much more. It stores memories and experiences. It also makes it possible for you to think, learn, imagine, and feel all kinds of emotions.

The nerves from the body cross as they enter the brain. That means the right side of the brain controls the left side of your body. And the left side of the brain controls the right side of your body.

Speedy Fact 1

The brain is pinkish-gray and wrinkled—about the size of a large grapefruit.

Speedy Fact 2

Only very large animals have brains that weigh more than the human brain.

Speedy Fact 3

The brain makes up only two percent of the body's weight, but it uses 20 percent of the body's energy.

Speedy Fact 4

When you learn something new, the neurons in your brain make new connections—but your brain doesn't get any bigger.

Speedy Fact 5

The brain can remember about 100 billion bits of information. That's 500 times the number of facts in a set of encyclopedias.

Spinal Cord

The spinal cord carries information from nerves around the body to the brain. And it sends messages out through the nerves to the muscles.

The spinal cord also controls many automatic actions. If you touch a hot stove, your hand jerks away before you feel the pain. The spinal cord skips your brain and signals your muscle directly. This is called a reflex.

Speedy Fact 1

The spinal cord looks like a long, thick white rope. It is about 17 inches (44 cm) long, an inch (2.5 cm) wide, and weighs just over one ounce (28 g) in an average adult.

Speedy Fact 2

Scientists estimate that the spinal cord is made up of about one billion neurons.

Speedy Fact 3

If a person's spinal cord is torn or cut, he or she is paralyzed. That person cannot move or feel parts of the body below the damage.

THE SENSES
Sight

Your senses—sight, hearing, taste, smell, and touch—bring you information about the world around you.

Your eyes are the organs for seeing. Experts say that 80 percent of information that you get through your senses comes from your eyes. As you read this book, light bounces off the page and enters your eyeball. Inside, the lens forms pictures of the words on the back wall of your eye, called the retina. The retina is lined with millions of nerve cells. Each cell picks up a tiny bit of each letter and sends it to your brain. The brain then figures out what you are reading.

Speedy Fact 1

Eyeglasses help people whose eyeballs are too long or short to see better.

Speedy Fact 2

The retina has more than 260 million nerve cells—about 70 percent of all the body's nerve cells.

Speedy Fact 3

Your eye is called an eyeball because it's about the size and shape of a Ping-Pong ball—about an inch (2.5 cm) across.

Hearing

Your ears are the organs for hearing. The outer ears gather sound waves from the air and guide them into a long tube. The end of the tube is closed by a thin, tightly stretched covering of tissue called the eardrum.

The sound waves make the eardrum shake back and forth, or vibrate. The vibrations pass along to a row of three little bones—the hammer, anvil, and stirrup. The bones pass the sound waves to a tiny, coiled tube filled with liquid. Nerve endings in the liquid pick up the vibrations and send signals to your brain. And your brain lets you hear the sound.

Speedy Fact 1

The inner ear has no part in hearing. It gives us our sense of balance when sitting, standing, walking, or riding a bike.

Speedy Fact 2

The hammer, anvil, and stirrup are the smallest bones in the human body.

Speedy Fact 3

Doctors say, "Never put anything smaller than a football into your ears." That means never put *anything* into your ears—it may damage your hearing.

Speedy Fact 4

Humans can hear sounds higher than a flute's top note. But bats and dolphins can hear sounds even higher than that.

35

Touch

Your sense of touch works through the skin. The skin has millions of nerve cells for touch. These cells are in every part of your skin, from head to toe. Each responds to only one sensation—heat, cold, pain, touch, or pressure.

In some parts of your body, the nerve cells are far apart. In other places, the nerve cells are close together. Your fingertips, for example, have more nerve cells than any other spot on your skin. That's why you touch things with your fingers—not with your ears or nose!

Speedy Fact 1
Your hands have more than 1,300 nerve cells per square inch (6.5 cm²).

Speedy Fact 2
Your skin contains about three million nerve cells for pain. But don't try counting them!

Speedy Fact 3
Skin is the main organ of touch—but the tip of your tongue is even more sensitive.

Taste

Your tongue is the most sensitive part of your body. It is the main organ for taste. The surface is covered with many tiny bumps. Each one contains hundreds of nerve cells, called taste buds. They can pick up four flavors—sweet, salty, sour, and bitter.

Taste buds are scattered around. Some parts of the tongue have many nerves that taste sweet things. Other parts have nerves that taste sour, salty, or bitter things. But each kind of cell can taste only one flavor.

Speedy Fact 1

Humans have the most taste buds when they are young. They lose some as they grow older.

Speedy Fact 2

Not everything tastes the same to everyone. A substance that tastes sour to one person may taste bitter to someone else.

Speedy Fact 3

Taste buds work best when the food is wet.

Speedy Fact 4

Nerves in the tongue also tell you when there's a pit in a grape or if the soup's too hot.

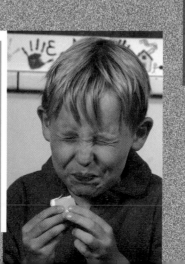

37

Smell

Your nose is for smelling. Most substances, from perfume to skunks, release odor molecules into the air. Each time you breathe in, some of these molecules enter your nose.

As the molecules move up your nose, they pass over millions of tiny nerve cells. These cells fire off signals to your brain. And your brain identifies the smell—perfume or skunk, hot dog or smoke, flowers or sweaty sneakers.

Speedy Fact 1

A human's sense of smell is not nearly as strong as a dog's. Your nose contains about five million smell cells. But a dog's nose can contain 200 million.

Speedy Fact 2

You can recognize more than 10,000 different smells.

Speedy Fact 3

Your sense of smell is far more sensitive than your sense of taste. You can smell one molecule of skunk odor mixed in with 30 billion molecules of air.

Speedy Fact 4

Generally speaking, women have a better sense of smell than men.

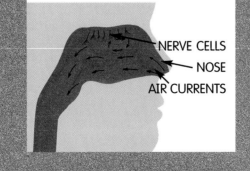

NERVE CELLS
NOSE
AIR CURRENTS

Speedy Fact 5

Your sense of smell works with your other senses. When you have a stuffy nose and can't smell very well, you can't taste the difference between an onion and an apple.

Other Senses

The five main senses of sight, hearing, touch, taste, and smell tell you what is happening near or far from your body. But did you know that you also have many other senses?

These other senses tell you what is happening inside your body. They pick up messages that flash through your body's nerve cells to your brain. These messages let you know whether you're hungry or thirsty, standing straight or leaning over, tired or peppy, and much, much more.

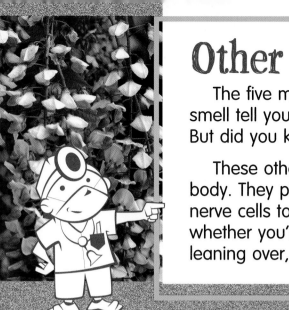

Speedy Fact 1

Nerve cells in the body let you touch the tip of your nose with your finger—even with your eyes closed.

Speedy Fact 2

Spinning around makes you dizzy because the fluid in your inner ear keeps whirling around, even after you stop spinning.

Speedy Fact 3

Disease, damage, or injury to a body part sends signals to your brain so that you feel pain.

SKIN
It's a Wrap

Your skin is an organ that covers your entire body. It is always growing. Old skin cells die. New skin cells take their place.

The thin, strong outer layer of the skin is the epidermis. It is mostly made of dead skin cells. The epidermis is only as thick as a sheet of paper and has no blood vessels. That's why a slight cut or scrape may hurt, but it rarely bleeds.

The much thicker inside layer of the skin, the dermis, has many blood vessels and nerve cells. When a cut or scrape hurts and bleeds, you know it has reached the dermis.

CLOSE-UP OF SKIN

Speedy Fact 1

Even though your skin is waterproof, some water does seep through. That's why skin wrinkles when swimming or bathing.

Speedy Fact 2

Every minute, about 50,000 tiny bits of dead skin fall off your body. About 75 percent of the dust in your house is dead skin cells.

Speedy Fact 3

You lose as much as 3 gallons (11.4 l) of sweat on a hot day through more than two million sweat pores or openings.

Speedy Fact 4

Your skin is one third of an inch (0.8 cm) thick on your back but only one one-hundredth of an inch (0.03 cm) thick on your eyelids.

Cuts and Scratches

Deep cuts and scratches cause bleeding. But most heal in a few days. How does this happen?

Floating in the blood are the tiny disks called platelets. Platelets pile up around the cut. Chemicals in the platelets cause sticky threads to form. The threads weave a net that holds the platelets and other blood cells in place. The bleeding stops.

Soon a scab forms over the injury. New skin cells replace the damaged cells. In time, the scab falls off. The skin is as good as new.

Speedy Fact 1

Pus is made up mostly of white blood cells and bits of dead skin from the wound.

Speedy Fact 2

When a scab falls off, the skin looks pink because it is still quite thin. When the skin grows back to its full thickness, the skin becomes the same color as the rest of your body.

Speedy Fact 3

Skin infections are caused by germs inside the wound that give off poisons, making the skin turn red and feel hot.

Hair

Hair is mostly shafts of dead skin cells. The only living part of hair—the root—is inside the skin.

Hair can be straight, wavy, or curly depending on the shape of the shaft. Straight hair has a round shape. Wavy hair is oval. Curly hair is flat.

The color of hair comes from a chemical called melanin. Pure melanin makes hair brown or black. If the melanin contains iron, the hair is blond. Hair that contains sulfur is red. As people grow older, their hair contains less coloring matter, and it turns gray or white.

Speedy Fact 1
Haircuts don't hurt because only dead cells are clipped.

Speedy Fact 2
Each hair grows nearly 5 inches (12.7 cm) a year.

Speedy Fact 3
The longest hair on record belonged to Ho Sateow of Thailand. He did not have a haircut for 70 years and his hair was 16 feet, 11 inches (5.15 m) long.

Speedy Fact 4
Hair is very strong. A single hair can hold a 3-ounce (84 g) weight. Weave a rope of 10,000 hairs and it can pick up an automobile.

Speedy Fact 5
Hair grows faster in children than adults, faster in the morning than at night, and faster in summer than in winter.

Speedy Fact 6
About 100 hairs fall out every day. But don't worry—you have about 100,000 hairs on your head.

1 If never cut, your finger-nails would grow to a length of nearly 12 feet (366 cm).

Nails

Fingernails and toenails are like hair in a few ways. Both are made of dead skin cells. The only living parts are under the skin. They are always growing. And neither hurt when you cut them.

Strong and stiff, your nails protect your fingers and toes. The fingernails also help you peel, scrape, and scratch itches. It takes the body about five months to grow a full-length fingernail.

2 Romesh Sharma, is listed in the *Guinness Book of World Records* as having the longest fingernails in the world. This is how his nails looked on June 8, 2000. Sharma protects his nails with green tape to keep them from breaking while he is traveling.

HUMAN AND ANIMAL "NAILS"

HUMAN NAILS

BEAR CLAWS

HORSE HOOVES

HAWK TALONS

3 Fingernails grow about 1.5 inches (3.8 cm) a year. Toenails grow only one inch (2.5 cm) in the same time.

GROWTH
Birth to Full-grown

You started life as a single cell—smaller than the head of a pin. This cell divided and became two cells. The two cells divided and became four cells. The cells kept on dividing and dividing until there were about ten trillion cells.

After about nine months, all the cells had joined together in tissues, organs, and organ systems. You had become a baby, ready to be born.

From birth until today, your cells continued to divide. More cells mean a bigger body. When you are about 18 years old or so, the dividing will stop. You will be fully grown.

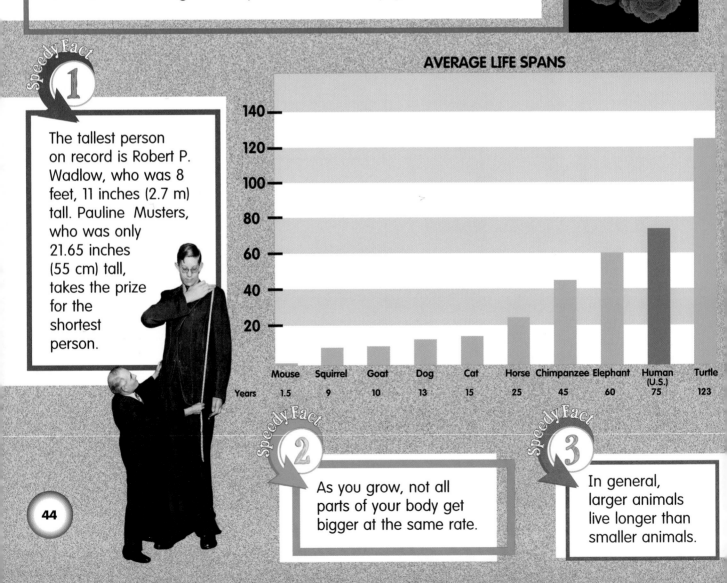

Speedy Fact 1

The tallest person on record is Robert P. Wadlow, who was 8 feet, 11 inches (2.7 m) tall. Pauline Musters, who was only 21.65 inches (55 cm) tall, takes the prize for the shortest person.

AVERAGE LIFE SPANS

	Mouse	Squirrel	Goat	Dog	Cat	Horse	Chimpanzee	Elephant	Human (U.S.)	Turtle
Years	1.5	9	10	13	15	25	45	60	75	123

Speedy Fact 2

As you grow, not all parts of your body get bigger at the same rate.

Speedy Fact 3

In general, larger animals live longer than smaller animals.

Heredity

You look a little like your parents—same skin color, hair, eyes, height, shape of ears or nose, way of walking or talking—because of heredity (huh-RED-uh-tee). Heredity is the passing on of traits from parents to children.

The original cell that develops into a human being contains all the instructions needed for that person to live and grow. The instructions are found in tiny parts of the cell called genes. One set of genes comes from the mother; the other set comes from the father.

As a baby grows, the mother's genes control some features and the father's genes control others. Certain features are controlled by genes from both the father and mother. This explains why children look a little like their parents—but never exactly the same.

Speedy Fact 1

Identical twins grow from a single egg and have the exact same genes. Such births occur in about four out of every 1,000 times.

Speedy Fact 2

Whether you are born a boy or girl depends on your genes.

Speedy Fact 3

The gene for brown eyes is stronger than the gene for blue eyes. If one parent has brown eyes and the other blue eyes, most of the children in the family will have brown eyes.

Speedy Fact 4

Fraternal twins grow from two different eggs and have different genes. Unlike identical twins, fraternal twins may be one boy and one girl.

Keeping Fit

Your body is like a machine. But in one important way it's different: Machines can break down from too much use. But your body only grows stronger with use and exercise.

Exercise strengthens your heart, lungs, and muscles, and improves your circulation. It keeps you healthy and may help you live longer. Keeping fit also requires good food, fresh air, plenty of rest and sleep, and regular visits to the doctor.

Among the best exercises are jogging, bicycling, and swimming. Playing active sports a few times a week and frequent walks also count as exercise.

Speedy Fact 1

Exercise makes your muscles bigger, stronger, and able to work longer without tiring.

Speedy Fact 2

During exercise, your heart pumps more blood and your lungs take in more air.

Speedy Fact 3

You sweat during exercise because muscles produce heat when they work.

Eating Right

Your body uses food in several ways. Some food is slowly burned to produce energy for your muscles and other body cells. Some food is used to make new cells.

The energy foods include bread, rice, pasta, fats, oils, sugar, and starch. Meat, milk, fish, and eggs are foods that are especially good for making new cells in the body. They also supply some energy.

Vitamins and minerals help to build bones and teeth and make red blood cells. They are found in such foods as fruit, vegetables, milk, and grains. Also, water is a very important part of your diet. Water dissolves foods, carries away waste products, and helps cool the body.

Speedy Fact 1

You can go several weeks without food. But you can only go about six days without water.

Speedy Fact 2

You need about 2 quarts (1.9 l) of water a day. You can get it by drinking water, drinking beverages that contain water, or by eating foods that contain a lot of water.

Speedy Fact 3

You eat nearly a half ton (0.5 t) of food in a year. That's like eating 4,000 quarter-pound (113 g) hamburgers.

HOW MUCH WATER DO FOODS CONTAIN?

100%	
75%	
50%	
25%	

Tomato	Watermelon	Apple	Potato	Bread
95%	93%	85%	80%	36%

A VISIT TO THE DOCTOR

Since you were born, you have probably visited your doctor many times for checkups. Each checkup is pretty much the same. What are these checkups all about?

First, the doctor usually measures your height and weight. This is to make sure you are growing at a normal rate.

Then the doctor presses on different parts of your body. Are the bones lined up right? Do all the organs feel healthy?

Using a small penlight, the doctor checks your eyes, ears, nose, and throat. Then the doctor listens to your heart and lungs with a stethoscope. Thumping and tapping your chest tells the doctor about the size and location of these organs.

Sometimes the doctor uses an X-ray machine to see inside your body. The checkup may also include a blood test, which the doctor studies for the cells and chemicals it contains. Finally, the doctor may give you a "shot" to prevent certain diseases.

Going for regular checkups is a good way to safeguard your health. You cannot know as much about your body as your doctor does. But you can learn how your body works. And you can work to keep it healthy.